KOALAS

Jen Green

Grolier
an imprint of
█SCHOLASTIC
www.scholastic.com/librarypublishing

Published 2009 by Grolier
An imprint of Scholastic Library Publishing
Old Sherman Turnpike, Danbury,
Connecticut 06816

For The Brown Reference Group plc
Project Editor: Jolyon Goddard
Picture Researcher: Clare Newman
Designers: Dave Allen, Jeni Child, Lynne Ross,
 Sarah Williams
Managing Editors: Bridget Giles, Tim Harris

Volume ISBN-13: 978-0-7172-6299-1
Volume ISBN-10: 0-7172-6299-5

**Library of Congress
Cataloging-in-Publication Data**

Nature's children. Set 4.
 p. cm.
 Includes bibliographical references and
 index.
 ISBN 13: 978-0-7172-8083-4
 ISBN 10: 0-7172-8083-7 ((set 4) : alk. paper)
 1. Animals--Encyclopedias, Juvenile. 1.
 Grolier (Firm)
 QL49.N385 2009
 590.3--dc22

 2007046315

Printed and bound in China

PICTURE CREDITS

Front Cover: **Shutterstock**: Gianna
Stadelmyer.

Back Cover: **Nature PL**: Laurent Geslin;
Photolibrary.com: JTB Photo;
Shutterstock: Troy Casswell, Holger Mette.

Ardea: D. Parer and E. Parer-Cook 41;
Corbis: Martin Harvey/Gallo Images 38;
Nature PL: John Cancalosi 9, 10, Laurent
Geslin 17, 21, Stephen David Miller 46, Dave
Watts 45. **Photolibrary.com**: Daniel Cox
42, Bill Schildge 37; **Shutterstock**: John
Austin 6, Blewis Photography 30, Troy
Casswell 13, Francois Etienne Du Plessis 18,
Kaspars Grinvalds 29, Eric Isselee 4, 5, Merryl
McNaughton 14, Hans Meerbeck 34, Holger
Mette 33, Walter Quirtmair 2–3, Ian Scott
26–27, Shutterspeed Images 22.

Contents

FACT FILE: Koalas

Class	Mammals (Mammalia)
Order	Koalas, possum, wombats, kangaroos, cuscuses, and brushtails (Diprotodontia)
Family	Phascolarctidae
Genus	*Phascolarctos* (one species)
Species	Koala (*Phascolarctos cinerus*)
World distribution	Eastern Australia
Habitat	Eucalyptus forests
Distinctive physical characteristics	The fur is gray or reddish, with paler fur on the belly; round ears; black leathery nose; the feet have long claws; females have a pouch on their belly
Habits	Live alone; spend much of their time asleep or feeding; active at night
Diet	Eucalyptus leaves

Introduction

With its tufty ears and large black nose, the koala is one of the most familiar **mammals**. Koalas live in the forests of Australia, where they spend most of their time snoozing high in the treetops. These animals are sometimes called "koala bears," because of their bearlike shape. However, koalas are not related to other bears, such as pandas and grizzlies.

The word *koala* comes from an Australian Aboriginal word meaning "does not drink water." True to its name, the koala gets most of the water it needs from its food—the leaves of evergreen trees called eucalyptus—so they rarely need to drink.

Koalas have a very firm grip. That is very helpful because the bark of their eucalyptus-tree homes can be smooth and slippery.

5

A joey digs its claws deep into its mother's fur as it rides on her back.

Fluffy Cub

Young koalas are called cubs, or joeys. Each female koala only has one cub at a time. The joey looks like a miniature version of its mother, only fluffier.

At about six months old, the joey spends much of its time riding on its mother's back as she moves through the trees in search of food. The cub also does some exploring on its own, but its mother is never very far away. When the joey feels lost or lonely, it cries for its mother. A young koala's cries sound a lot like the noises a human baby makes when it is hungry, tired, or uncomfortable. The young koala continues to depend on its mother until it is about one year old.

Pouched Mammals

When is a bear not a bear? When it is a koala bear! Koalas look a lot like bears, but they actually belong to a completely different group of animals—the pouched mammals, or **marsupials**. The koala's relatives include kangaroos, wallabies, and opossum. The sleepy-looking wombats are the koala's closest relatives. There are many types, or **species**, of kangaroos and wallabies, but only one living species of koala.

Young pouched mammals develop differently from other young mammals. They are born at a very early stage of development. When born, they are tiny and hairless, with only stumps for back legs. Baby koalas and most other young marsupials finish developing inside a pouch on their mother's belly. Female kangaroos and wallabies have a pouch with the opening at the top—like a pocket. Female koalas and wombats raise their joeys in a pouch with the opening at the bottom.

This young joey has ventured out of its mother's pouch to take a look around.

Another species of koala used to live in Australia. It died out 50,000 years ago for unknown reasons.

Life Down Under

Most marsupials live in Australia and the surrounding islands. Koalas once lived throughout most of the vast island continent. Today, they are only found in eastern Australia.

Koalas live in eucalyptus forests that provide their leafy food. Almost all of eastern Australia was once covered in forest. However, today much of these forests have been cut down. With fewer eucalyptus trees to live in, there are now fewer koalas living in the wild.

The forests of northeastern Australia are hot and steamy. The koalas that live there have reddish fur that is thin and fine. Farther south, the climate is cooler. The koalas of southeastern Australia have longer, thicker fur than northern koalas. Southeastern koalas are also larger—the extra bulk helps keep them warm.

Portrait of a Koala

It's difficult to confuse a koala with any other animal. The broad, rounded head and black, leathery nose are unmistakable. The large, round ears are fringed with long hair. The eyes are sleepy and blinking.

Koalas have a stocky, rounded body. The tail is very short and stumpy. Their woolly fur makes them look soft and cuddly. These powerful animals have strong, muscular legs, which allow them to climb trees with ease.

Male koalas grow to 31 inches (78 cm) long and weigh up to 30 pounds (14 kg). That's about as much as a three-year-old child. The females are usually smaller and about two-thirds the weight of the males.

In addition to being larger, male koalas have a broader face and smaller ears than females.

13

In the early 20th century, millions of koalas were killed for their fur.

14

Furry Body

The koala's scientific name is *Phascolarctos cinerus* (FASS-koll-ark-toss SIN-uh-rus). That means "ash-colored pouched bear." However, as mentioned earlier, northern koalas are often reddish rather than ash-colored, or grayish.

The fur on a koala's head, back, and the outside of its legs is darker than the hair on the chest and belly. The fur on the insides of the legs, inside the ears, and on the chin is also pale. This mottled coloring helps disguise the koala as it climbs through the trees. Any animal looking up finds it hard to notice the koala among the dappled leaves and grayish bark of the eucalyptus trees. This natural disguise is called **camouflage**. It helps protect a koala from its enemies.

Treetop Home

A koala spends almost all its life high up among the eucalyptus trees. It eats, sleeps, **mates**, and even gives birth among the branches—rarely descending to the ground. Being comfortable at great heights and having good balance mean that the koala is safe even when high winds rock the trees.

When moving from tree to tree, the koala climbs along a slender branch until the limb bends and touches the next tree. The branch serves as a bridge between trees, allowing the koala to find a fresh supply of leaves to eat. When climbing upward, the koala hugs the trunk with its front paws. The back legs push upward while the front paws slide up the tree.

A koala has such a
good technique for
climbing that it can
scale a tree with
little effort.

A koala's sharp claws
are made of a tough
substance called keratin.

Nimble Paws

Koalas have strong front-leg and shoulder muscles—ideal for clinging onto trees. Their feet are also perfectly designed for climbing. All four paws have a rough sole, which helps the animal grip onto tree bark. They also have long, curving claws that dig into the bark.

Like humans, koalas have five **digits** on each foot. Each front paw has two thumblike digits that can press against the other digits. That gives the koala a particularly good grip on slippery branches. The back feet have one thumb each. The fourth and fifth digits have stout claws for grasping. The second and third digits are joined to make a comb, which the koala uses to clean, or groom, its fur.

On the Ground

Sooner or later, a koala has to climb down to the ground to move between clumps of trees. The koala also descends to eat soil and gravel, which help it break down, or digest, its food. The koala carefully climbs down feet-first, reversing the movements that it made to climb up the tree.

On the ground, a koala is in danger of being attacked by **predators** such as dingoes—a type of wild dog. The wary koala moves as fast as it can, consuming mouthfuls of soil, before heading to the safety of the nearest tree.

The koala can also swim quite well. It paddles across creeks with just the top part of its head showing above water. Once back on land, the animal shakes itself energetically. Water drops fly everywhere, and it is soon dry again.

On the ground, koalas
walk slowly on all fours.

Dingoes are wild dogs
that came to Australia
with human settlers
thousands of years ago.
They eat many animals,
including koalas.

Koalas in Danger

Koalas might look cuddly and harmless, but they can certainly put up a fight if cornered. They will bite with their sharp teeth, kick with their powerful legs, and scratch with their strong, curved claws.

In the wild, koalas are often **prey** for ground-dwelling predators such as foxes, dingoes, and large lizards. High in the trees there are fewer threats to adult koalas. But young koalas can be snatched by wedge-tailed eagles that swoop low over the treetops. In the past, people also hunted koalas, both for their meat and their soft fur. Fortunately, hunting koalas is now against the law.

Night Senses

The animal kingdom can be divided into two main types of creatures—**diurnal** and **nocturnal**. Diurnal animals are active during the day, and nocturnal animals are active at night. Koalas are nocturnal. They are most active in the hours just after sunset.

Like many nocturnal animals, the koala's most developed senses are smell and hearing. Its nose is so sensitive that it can identify the different kinds of eucalyptus leaves just by standing at the base of the tree. It can also easily tell if any other koalas are nearby. The large, round ears channel sounds to aid its hearing. For diurnal animals such as humans, eyesight is often the most utilized sense. Sight is less important to koalas, which is a good thing for them as their small eyes do not see very well.

Picky Eaters

Koalas eat almost nothing but the leaves of eucalyptus trees. There are many different types of eucalyptus trees, and koalas do not eat the leaves of all of them. A koala uses its super-sensitive nose to tell if a eucalyptus is one with leaves it can eat. Even when it finds the right type of tree, it must still be careful. Young eucalyptus leaves contain poisons that can kill a careless koala. The animal must sniff each twig carefully to make sure the leaves are not harmful before munching away.

The koala uses the sharp teeth at the front of its mouth to cut the leaves off the branches. Broad, blunt back teeth called **molars** are used to crush the tough, fibrous leaves to a pulp. If the koala comes upon a good source of food, it can store leaves in its stretchy cheek pouches for later.

For their size, koalas have on average a tiny brain. It weighs just 0.6 ounces (17 g)—0.2 percent of the koala's total body weight. In contrast, a human's brain weighs about 2 percent of their total body weight.

Cough Drops?

Few other animals compete with the koala for food. Most animals cannot eat eucalyptus leaves because they are tough to digest and contain poisons. Koalas have a digestive system specially designed to digest the leaves. A portion of the digestive system, called the cecum (SEE-cum), is very long in koalas—about 8 feet (2.5 m). In the cecum, **microscopic** germs break up the tough fibers of the eucalyptus leaves. That allows the koala to absorb as many nutrients as possible from the tough plants. The koala's digestive system also makes the poisons safe.

Strong-smelling oils in eucalyptus leaves make koalas smell like cough drops! This smell is not very pleasant, but it does have a useful purpose. Fleas, ticks, and other parasites—tiny animals that feed on the blood of koalas and other animals—don't like the smell either. So eating eucalyptus leaves actually helps keep pesky bugs away.

The koala's liver breaks down the poisons in eucalyptus leaves, making them safe to eat.

29

A koala that lives for 16 years would spend 12 of those years asleep!

30

Sleepyheads

If there is one thing koalas are famous for it's sleeping! Once the Sun has set, a koala spends a few hours feeding. When its belly is full, the koala dozes off and spends the rest of the night asleep. On average, a koala sleeps for about 18 hours each day.

It may seem like the sleepyheads are being lazy, but dozing is a natural way of saving energy. Eucalyptus leaves aren't very nourishing, and they require a lot of energy to digest. So the koala saves energy by resting and also by moving about at a snail's pace. Sometimes, a koala will even doze off in the middle of eating, with leaves hanging from its mouth!

What a Scorcher!

In Australia, temperatures can really heat up in summer. The thin leaves of eucalyptus trees provide only light, dappled shade. If the day is a real scorcher, the koala may move to a leafier tree that provides dense shade, before dozing off.

Koalas can fall asleep in almost any position— stretched along a branch or with their arms wrapped around the trunk. They may snooze in the fork of a tree with their head resting on a branch. A pad of thick skin on the animal's backside acts as a cushion, helping make its perch much more comfortable. In really hot weather, koalas eat less and spend even more time resting in the shade.

When it's really hot, a koala licks its legs. As the saliva dries, it cools the animal. Koalas can't sweat to keep cool, like humans.

33

Koalas feed from about 30 different types of eucalyptus trees. They occasionally eat the leaves of other types of trees, such as acacias.

Keep Out!

Unlike many animals, koalas do not have a regular **den** or nest where they sleep each night. They don't even have a favorite tree to sleep in. However, they do have a **territory**— a home patch where they feed and sleep. The female koala's territory covers about 2½ acres (1 ha). Male koalas have a bigger territory, which usually overlaps with the territories of several females.

Koalas are mainly solitary animals. Except during the **breeding season**, they do not like to share their territory with others. If another koala approaches the tree where the animal is resting, the koala in the tree growls a warning. That tells the intruder to move on—or there might be a fight.

Noisy Neighbors

Koalas are quiet while they are asleep—but when they wake up, they can get noisy! They make all sorts of sounds to communicate with other koalas. Some noises mean "Come closer!" Other sounds mean "Back off!" Male koalas make harsh grating noises that sound like a saw cutting through wood. Those sounds warn other males to keep away from their territory.

Mating time is the noisy season for koalas. A male in search of a mate makes low roars, bellows, and mewing sounds. He can also produce a noise like a sneeze and a loud ticking sound like a clock! If any nearby female is in the mood for mating, she answers with her own roars and croons. The two animals follow the direction of the sounds to find each other.

A koala's
loud call
can be heard
from more
than half a mile
(1 km) away.

After mating, a male koala leaves a female to raise the joey on her own.

Time to Breed

Spring and summer are the breeding season for koalas—that's September to February in Australia. At this time, male koalas wander the far corners of their territory in search of a mate. The male rubs a smelly scent that comes from a **gland** on his chest onto trees at the edge of his territory. This scent warns other males to keep away. Any male koala that ignores the warning signs and enters, does so at his own risk. The two will fight, biting and scratching at each other. In most cases, the challenger loses and wanders off.

Once a male and female meet and get to know each other, they will mate. The male returns to his solitary way of life immediately after mating.

Born Early

Female koalas usually give birth to a single joey every other year. Occasionally, they have twins. Before the baby is born, the mother prepares its future home—the pouch—by giving it a good spring cleaning. She licks a little trail for the baby to follow to the pouch.

Koalas joeys are born just 35 days after their parents mate. That's a very short time for a mammal of this size. Like other marsupials, the baby enters the world at a very early stage of development. A newborn koala is pink, hairless, and not much larger than a bee. Its back legs are only stumps, but its front legs are better developed. With its front legs, the baby claws its way upward through its mother's fur, using a swimming motion. Instinctively, the joey heads straight for the pouch and scrambles inside.

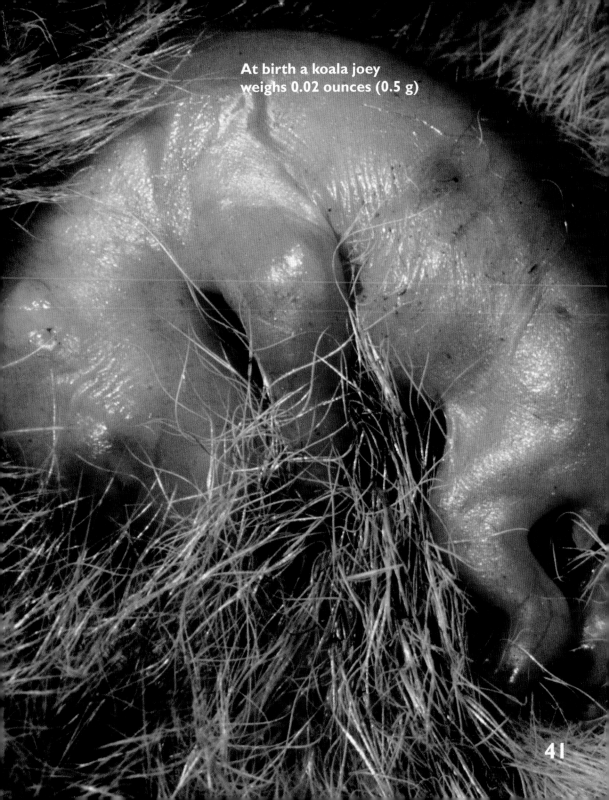

At birth a koala joey
weighs 0.02 ounces (0.5 g)

A female koala
has two teats in her
pouch that provide
milk for the joey.

Snug in the Pouch

Once inside the pouch, the baby koala clamps onto a teat and begins to **suckle** its mother's rich milk. The teat swells to fill the joey's mouth. That way, the young koala cannot fall out of the pouch as its mother scrambles through the trees.

The young koala continues its development in the safety of the pouch. Eventually, its eyes and ears open and its fur begins to grow. Its tiny legs gradually get bigger and stronger. After a few weeks, the joey is able to let go of the teat without falling out of the pouch, but it continues to suckle. It will be many more weeks before it is ready to begin exploring the outside world.

Hitching a Ride

At six or seven months old, the joey is ready to leave the pouch and go out into the big, wide world. At first the joey is a little hesistant to explore its new world, and the young koala often climbs straight back into the pouch! However, the joey eventually grows bolder. Soon it is spending more and more time outside its mother's pouch in the leafy world of the eucalyptus trees.

At about the age of eight months, the baby returns to the pouch only to sleep. When it is not sleeping, it hitches a ride on its mother's back as she climbs through the treetops. That is a lot more comfortable than riding in the pouch, because when the mother leaps from tree to tree, she lands on her pouch. That can give the joey quite a thump!

Oils from the eucalyptus leaves that koalas eat come out of their skin and condition their fur, making it waterproof like a raincoat.

Koalas have a large nose—their sense of smell is about ten times as powerful as that of humans.

Changing Diet

Throughout its time in the pouch, the joey is nourished by its mother's milk. At about five months old, the joey tries solid food. The gradual replacement of milk for solid food is called **weaning**. Among the baby's first solid foods are its mother's droppings. These contain digested leaves that are safe for the baby to eat. They also contain microscopic germs from the mother's intestines, which will help the baby digest its own food.

Eucalyptus leaves may smell like cough drops to humans, but to the joey their smell becomes irresistible. By about one year old, it has been weaned off its mother's milk and is feeding on only eucalyptus leaves.

Growing Up

The joey sticks close to its mother for the first year of its life. If danger threatens or the joey feels tired, it tries to climb back into the pouch. Eventually the mother has had enough. She makes it clear to her cub that it is too old for the pouch. For young males, this is when they know it is time to leave and set up their own territory. Young females are usually allowed to stay closer to home. Young males may start to breed at the age of four years, females at just two years old.

In some parts of eastern Australia, koalas became scarce in the mid-20th century because so many eucalyptus trees had been cut down. Many koalas were also killed for their fur. In addition, many koalas died of diseases spread from domestic animals. Luckily, people realized in time that the animal was disappearing, and they took steps to save the koala. Now many Australians are helping to ensure that these unique animals continue to live a sleepy but contented life in the wild.

Words to Know

Breeding season   The time of year when a type of animal mates.

Camouflage   Special patterns and colors that make an animal difficult to see against a particular background.

Den   The home of an animal such as a fox.

Digits   Fingers, thumbs, or toes.

Diurnal   Active during daylight hours.

Gland   A part of the body that produces a liquid, such as sweat or saliva.

Mammals   Warm-blooded animals with fur or hair that feed their young on milk.

Marsupials   Mammals whose young are born early and complete their development in a pouch on the mother's belly.

Mates   Comes together to produce young.

Microscopic   So small that it can be seen only by using a microscope.

Molars   The broad back teeth that are used for chewing and grinding food.

Nocturnal   Active at night.

Predators   Animals that hunt other animals.

Prey   An animal eaten by another animal.

Species   The scientific word for animals of the same kind that can breed together.

Suckle   To drink milk from the mother.

Territory   An area an animal lives in and which it defends against others of its kind.

Weaning   The time when a young mammal switches from milk to solid food.

Find Out More

Books

Kalman, Bobbie. *The Life Cycle of a Koala*. Minneapolis, Minnesota: Tandem Library, 2002.

Riley, J. *Koalas*. Early Bird Nature Books. Minneapolis, Minnesota: Lerner Publications, 2005.

Web sites

Creature Feature: Koalas
kids.nationalgeographic.com/Animals/CreatureFeature/Koala
A ton of information and pictures of koalas.

Koala
enchantedlearning.com/subjects/mammals/marsupial/Koalaprintout.shtml
Facts and a printout of a koala to color in.

Index